VIEW-MASTER LAND

poem by

Matt Bialer

Finishing Line Press
Georgetown, Kentucky

VIEW-MASTER LAND

*This is for my new love, Mary Kathleen Flynn.
It's always sunrises and sunsets being with you.
Always magic. I love you.*

Copyright © 2023 by Matt Bialer
ISBN 979-8-88838-317-9 First Edition
All rights reserved under International and Pan-American Copyright Conventions. No part of this book may be reproduced in any manner whatsoever without written permission from the publisher, except in the case of brief quotations embodied in critical articles and reviews.

Publisher: Leah Huete de Maines
Editor: Christen Kincaid
Cover Art: Matt Bialer
Author Photo: Mary Kathleen Flynn
Cover Design: Elizabeth Maines McCleavy

Order online: www.finishinglinepress.com
also available on amazon.com

Author inquiries and mail orders:
Finishing Line Press
PO Box 1626
Georgetown, Kentucky 40324
USA

The long poem VIEW-MASTER LAND is about the poet's struggle to come to terms with the loss of his wife Lenora and the profound changes to his life that her death has brought. It's also about celebrating companionship and hope with his new love, Mary. It's about how technology like the BlackBerry, which seemed so wondrous when it was first introduced, is now defunct, a relic of the past. It's about the act of seeing, and how that evolves and gains depth as we get older. Bialer shares his memories of the View-Master toy he grew up with and how magical it was to view his favorite childhood TV shows in three dimensions on a special-format stereoscope and corresponding "reels," which are thin cardboard disks. There was even an attempt to bring the View-Master back in cutting-edge VR technology, but that too failed, underscoring its obsolescence. VIEW-MASTER LAND is about how our perception is enhanced as we go through life, and how the most ordinary can become extraordinary.

Today
January 3rd
Is the 22 month anniversary
Of being with my girlfriend
Mary
22 months
We met right before
Covid lockdown

Later
This afternoon
I will meet her
For lunch
To celebrate
The New Year
As well as
Our wonderful months
Together

I also see the news
That the classic
BlackBerry phone
Is being forced
To retire
"Put out to pasture"

A pioneer
Of the
On-the-go email
Paragon of
Corporate correctness

It reigned supreme
In the days
When physical keyboards
Had yet to yield
To touch screens

But come tomorrow
The BlackBerry
Will become
One more relic
Of a bygone era
As the transition
To 5G wireless technology
Moves forward

One more relic
Of a bygone era

After its
"End of life date"
As BlackBerry calls it
Devices running on
BlackBerry's legacy
Operating systems
And software
"Will no longer
Reliably function"

Old devices
Won't be able
To send text messages
Or dial 911

Placing them firmly
In the realm
Of floppy disks
And rotary phones

One more relic
Of a bygone era

Will no longer
Reliably function

It's now
32 months
After you died
And I'm doing better
Than I was before

More time has gone by

I once read
That when a loved one dies
They don't die
Just once
But a thousand times
A thousand times

The death
Of BlackBerry
Is another death
Of you

Even though
You had long ago
Switched
From BlackBerry
To the iPhone
You made
The switch
Kicking and screaming

You loved
Your BlackBerry
You got a smart phone
Before me
And at the time
I was always baffled
By how much time
You spent on it
Addicted
But always
For work

When the iPhone came
You resisted
You didn't care
About touch screens
Or web surfing
You had trouble typing
On a touchscreen keyboard
But you had no choice
It was tough luck
Your work

Was making the transition
Out of BlackBerry

More time has gone by

For me
It was good riddance
To the BlackBerry
I hated
That rolling ball
That would
Get stuck with lint

I was always
Dipping a Q-tip
In rubbing alcohol
To get the lint out
And most of the time
It didn't work

I must've
Gone through
Five BlackBerrys
While you
Still used
Your cherished first one

The death
Of BlackBerry
Is another death
Of you

Makes me
Feel like
You're one more relic
And so is
Our 31 years together

More time has gone by

Your last iPhone
Was shut off
And sits stored away
In a closet
In our house
32 months later

One more relic
Of a bygone era

Will no longer
Reliably function

Even our
Entire old way
Of life
Might be
Another relic
Another death

With the Covid-19 pandemic
We thought perhaps
That we were finally

Out of the woods
Out of the woods

But now
There's the Omicron variant
And it might
Be a more mild form
Of Covid-19
But it is
Far more contagious

The United States
Has far surpassed
The number of
Daily Covid infections
Compared with
The previous peak
Last winter
Yet many businesses
Remain open
Stadiums are packed
And children
Are headed
Back to school
After the winter holidays

Some news headlines announce
That "Omicron infections
Seem to be milder"
Than earlier variants
Yet this could be

"The worst public health challenge
Of our lifetimes"

The individual risk
Is low
With vaccinated
And boosted people
There is a steep price
To keeping students
Out of school
Shuttering restaurants
And retail shops
Stopping travel
And commerce

And yet
So many firefighters
And emergency medical personnel
Are out
Because of Covid
That Cincinnati declared
A state of emergency
One in 6 police officers
In New York City
Has symptoms
Or was diagnosed
With Covid
Last week
Thousands of flights
Have been canceled
Because of inadequate staffing

Hospital resources
Are stretched
To their maximum

Even our
Entire old way
Of life
Might be
Another relic
Another death

More time has gone by

My friend Allison
Posts on Facebook
A photo
Of an old View-Master
With the caption
"How I used
To scroll through pictures
Before Instagram"

One more relic
Of a bygone era

When I was a kid
I used to love
View-Master

View-Master

The first one
Made its debut
At the 1939 World's Fair
In New York City
It was a marvel
Cutting edge

A compact
Modern stereoscopic device
Designed for viewing
Three-dimensional
Full-color
Picture transparencies
Mounted in
View-Master reels

Opens a new world
Of exciting
Educational adventure
Through the magic dimensions
Of living stereo color

Youngsters
Will visit
Far-away lands
See wild animals
Thrill to true-life adventures
Laugh with cartoon favorites
See fairy tale characters
That seem almost real

Almost real

The View-Master
Is slightly larger
Than a pair of opera glasses
Precision-built
Of stainless steel
And hard plastic

Each View-Master reel
Is on treated paper
In which is mounted
Seven stereoscopic sets
Of full-color
Kodachrome pictures
When seen through
The View-Master
These sets
Appear as
Seven realistic
Three-dimensional pictures

I remember
Marveling
At 20,000 LEAGUES UNDER THE SEA

Yogi Bear
Bugs Bunny
Donald Duck

Every boy and girl
Will be thrilled
To see
Their cartoon favorites
And fairy tale pictures
"Come to life"
With the realism
Of View-Master
Full-color stereo pictures

My favorites
Were BATMAN
With Adam West
LAND OF THE GIANTS
And THE WORLD OF THE DINOSAURS

This is the way
To View-Master Land

One more relic
Of a bygone era

Will no longer
Reliably function

Placing them firmly
In the realm
Of floppy disks
And rotary phones

More time has gone by

About 7 years ago
They tried
To bring the View-Master
Back to life
Back to life

A virtual reality reboot

Google and Mattel
Teamed up
To produce
A plastic viewer
That pairs up
With our smart phone

Explore VR environments
Make three-dimensional dinosaurs
Appear real
Or
In classic fashion
Transport us
To faraway places
And historical monuments

Unlike the old View-Master's
Static images
We can spin around
In place

And see everything
Around us

But the new View-Master
Lasted only 4 years

One more relic
Of a bygone era

Will no longer
Reliably function

Placing it firmly
In the realm
Of floppy disks
Rotary phones
The old View-Master
Buster Brown shoes
And BlackBerry

The death
Of BlackBerry
Is another death
Of you

Even our
Entire old way
Of life
Might be
Another relic
Another death

More time has gone by

In the afternoon
I take the subway
From Park Slope
Brooklyn
To the Upper East Side
Manhattan
Where Mary lives

I will swing by
Her apartment
And we will walk
To Central Park
Where we have
A lunch reservation
At the Loeb Boathouse
One of the most
Famous icons
Of Central Park
And a place
Dear to our hearts

Located at
The northeastern tip
Of the lake
And houses
The Boathouse restaurant
A romantic setting
For dinner
Or lunch

We've watched
The sun sink
Behind the trees
And seen a gondola
Slowly poling past
And even
A Great Blue Heron
Fly by

Mary's still in
Full holiday mode
Long red coat
Of cashmere wool
With a green and gold
Holly pin on it
White cashmere sweater
Red, gray and white scarf
Mother of pearl necklace
That I got her for Christmas
And Roman glass earrings

She looks beautiful

Around 1874
Calvert Vaux
Designed
A two-story boathouse
The roof was a deck
To be covered
With awnings
Furnished with seats

The original structure
Served nobly
For 80 years
Until the 1950's
By which time
It was so run down
It had to be demolished

The current Boathouse
Took its place
In 1954

It features
Year-round dining
Overhead heating
To compensate
For the chilly winds
Of winter

We enter
Wearing masks
Show our ID
And proof
Of vaccination
We have a table
Overlooking the lake

It's winter now
No gondolas
Or herons
But we do see

A drone fly
Over the lake
Kind of creepy
"What's it doing?"
I ask Mary
"Probably filming
All of us"
"Let's wave hello"

We each order
The cream of potato and leek soup
And Mary orders
A chilled seafood salad
As her entrée
And I get the crab cake
We toast
The New Year
And Mary's new job
As editor-in-chief
Of PE Hub
A news source
About private equity

We talk
About the difficulties
We had
Bringing our daughters
Who are now both 19
Into this world
All of the medical issues

Which we've discussed
Many times before

Mary talks about
Her concern
For a relative's health
She's trying
To get updates

We order
Cheesecake
And Earl Grey tea
I tell her
I feel like
A relic
I can't drink coffee
The way I used to

And then
We go
For a walk
Even though
It's freezing out
We walk
Towards Bethesda Fountain
Gloves on
Holding hands

The sun
Is starting to set

It's windy
I joke
How I can't ski
In the cold anymore

I point
To the new skinny skyscrapers
That look like
Tall pencils
I tell Mary
How much I hate them

Mary jokes
"Every time we go
For a walk here
You always tell me
How much you hate them"

"I do
They've ruined
The classic New York skyline"

"Maybe you are
Indeed a relic"

We lock arms
We've gone on
So many walks
In Central Park
So many

And they're all lovely

Doesn't matter
How hot or cold
It is out

We fantasize
That if
We got married
It would
Have to be here
At the Boathouse
As Mary says
"It's ours"

"What month?"

Can't be a month
We were each
Married in before

We settle
On June

Mary adds
"I warn you
I'm traditional
When it comes
To this stuff
A formal proposal

A beautiful ceremony
White dress"

I tell her
She doesn't
Have to warn me
And I already know

Whatever
It is
It all
Has to be different
From our pasts

No relics

We can fantasize
At least for now

More time has gone by

Mary points
To the sunset
Over the Conservatory water
A pool in Central Park

Our mouths
Are agape

Mary says
"Oh
I gotta
Get some photos
Of this"

One of the things
I love about Mary
Is how she has
A deep connection
To the visual
It's visceral
Doesn't matter
How cold
Or windy it is
She'll go
For her iPhone

She is indeed
A view master

The sky
Is on fire
In the water
And behind the cityscape
Looming beyond it

Even my hated
Pencil skyscrapers
Look amazing

Luminous
Otherworldly
Like tall alien crystals

The sky
Is a beautiful
Fiery orange
Apocalyptic
Bright orange red

Wings of pink
And yellow and rose
Gold and crimson radiance

I feel like
It's the end
Of all things
The end of the world

But also
The magnificent beginning
Like Mary and I
The magnificent beginning

This is the way
To View-Master Land

Almost real

The sunset
Reminds me

Of a View-Master reel
I used to love
About THE WORLD OF THE DINOSAURS

Those seven images
The last ones
Of a Tyrannosaurus Rex
And a Triceratops
Locked in classic battle
My two favorite dinosaurs
I used to have
Action figures of them

But the sky
Is on fire
Like the fatal meteor
Just struck the earth
Just struck

But it looks glorious

Will no longer
Reliably function

They stop fighting
And curious
Just watch

Just watch

Matt **Bialer** is the author of more than a dozen books of poetry, including MAZE (Finishing Line Press), ALWAYS SAY GOODNIGHT (KYSO Flash), ASCENT (JournalStone) and THE VALLEY OF THE EIGHT and THIRD EYE OF THE INNER LIGHT (Leaky Boot Press). His poems have appeared in many print and online journals including *Cultural Weekly, Forklift Ohio, Green Mountains Review, H_NGM_N, Le Zaporogue* and *MacQueen's Quinterly.*

In addition, Matt is an acclaimed street photographer (primarily black and white) who has exhibited widely. Some of his images are held in the permanent collections of The Brooklyn Museum, The Museum of the City of New York and The New York Public Library. He is also an acclaimed watercolor landscape painter with works in many private collections and "best of" books. He lives in Park Slope, Brooklyn.

www.ingramcontent.com/pod-product-compliance
Lightning Source LLC
Chambersburg PA
CBHW022127090426
42743CB00008B/1047